SPORTS SUPERSTARS

WHO IS STEPHEN CURRY?

ZELDA WAGNER

Lerner Publications ◆ Minneapolis

Statistics in this book are accurate through the 2024–2025 National Basketball Association season.

Lerner Publications Company
An imprint of Lerner Publishing Group, Inc.
241 First Avenue North
Minneapolis, MN 55401 USA

For reading levels and more information, look up this title at www.lernerbooks.com.

Main body text set in Mikado.
Typeface provided by HvD Fonts.

Designer: Mary Ross **Photo Editor:** Evan Villas

Library of Congress Cataloging-in-Publication Data

Names: Wagner, Zelda, 2000- author
Title: Who is Stephen Curry? : Golden State Warriors superstar / Zelda Wagner.
Description: Minneapolis, MN : Lerner Publications, [2026] | Series: Sports superstars (lerner sports rookie) | Includes bibliographical references and index. | Audience: Ages 5–8 | Audience: Grades K–1 | Summary: "Golden State Warriors guard Stephen Curry changed the NBA with his three-point shooting. How did he become the greatest shooter in basketball history and win four NBA titles? Read about his life to find out"— Provided by publisher.
Identifiers: LCCN 2025020173 (print) | LCCN 2025020174 (ebook) | ISBN 9798765689622 library binding | ISBN 9798348029128 paperback | ISBN 9798765697900 epub
Subjects: LCSH: Curry, Stephen, 1988- —Juvenile literature | Golden State Warriors (Basketball team) —Juvenile literature | Basketball players—United States—Biography—Juvenile literature | Guards (Basketball) —United States—Biography—Juvenile literature | LCGFT: Biographies
Classification: LCC GV884.C88 W32 2026 (print) | LCC GV884.C88 (ebook) | DDC 796.323092 [B]—dc23/eng/20250708

LC record available at https://lccn.loc.gov/2025020173
LC ebook record available at https://lccn.loc.gov/2025020174

Manufactured in the United States of America
1-1012763-54830-7/22/2025

TABLE OF CONTENTS

Basketball's Best **4**

Stephen Curry Career Stats 22

Stephen Curry Gear 23

Glossary 24

Learn More 24

Index 24

BASKETBALL'S BEST

Stephen Curry jumped and shot the basketball. *Swish!* He scored three points for Team USA.

Stephen and Team USA were playing in the 2024 Olympic Games in Paris, France. They won the gold medal!

Stephen was born in Akron, Ohio, in 1988. His father, Dell Curry, played in the NBA.

Stephen worked hard to become a basketball star like his father.

But Stephen was smaller than many other players. He was often the smallest player on his team.

After high school, Stephen wanted to play college basketball. Some colleges thought he was too small.

He decided to go to Davidson College in North Carolina.

Stephen became a star at Davidson.

In 2008, Davidson had a great season. They reached the Elite Eight.

Stephen played one more season at Davidson. Then he was ready for the NBA.

In 2009, Stephen entered the NBA Draft.

The Golden State Warriors had the seventh pick in the draft. They chose Stephen.

Golden State had a losing record in Stephen's first three seasons. But the team got better.

In 2015, Stephen led Golden State to the NBA Finals. They beat the Cleveland Cavaliers!

It was Golden State's first NBA title in 40 years.

Stephen and Golden State won the title again in 2017, 2018, and 2022.

Stephen is an NBA champion. He is also the best three-point shooter in NBA history.

Stephen wants to win another NBA title. He has always worked hard to reach his goals.

STEPHEN CURRY

CAREER STATS

GAMES PLAYED: 1,062

POINTS: 25,386

THREE-POINT BASKETS: 4,058

ASSISTS: 6,540

NBA TITLES: 4

STEPHEN CURRY

GEAR

GLOSSARY

draft: when teams take turns choosing new players

Elite Eight: the final eight teams in the college basketball championship

NBA: National Basketball Association

title: championship

LEARN MORE

Leed, Percy. *Basketball's NBA and WNBA Finals*. Lerner Publications, 2025.

Streeter, Anthony. *NBA Finals All-Time Greats*. Press Box Books, 2025.

Wagner, Zelda. *Basketball Superstars*. Lerner Publications, 2025.

INDEX

Curry, Dell, 6

Davidson College, 10–13

Golden State Warriors, 15–19

NBA, 6, 13–14, 18, 20–21

NBA Finals, 17

PHOTO ACKNOWLEDGMENTS

Image credits: Meng Yongmin/Xinhua via Getty Images, p. 5; Doug Pensinger/Allsport/Getty Images, p. 7; Gregory Shamus/Getty Images, p. 9; Streeter Lecka/Getty Images, p. 11; Jeff Siner/Charlotte Observer/Tribune News Service via Getty Images, p. 12; Lance Iversen/San Francisco Chronicle via Getty Images, p. 15; MediaNews Group/Bay Area News via Getty Images, p. 17; Elsa/Getty Images, p. 19; Ronald Martinez/Getty Images, p. 20; Al Bello/Getty Images, p. 23. Design element: liangpv/Getty Images.
Cover: AP Photo/Loren Elliott.